THE GEORGIAN PLAYHOUSE

This is one of a Series of Illustrated Monographs on various aspects of Georgian Architecture and Decoration, at home and abroad. The Series is under the general editorship of the Publications Sub-Committee of the Georgian Group.

RICHARD SOUTHERN

THE GEORGIAN
PLAYHOUSE

LONDON
PLEIADES BOOKS LIMITED
1948

First published 1948
by Pleiades Books Ltd 11 Fitzroy Square London W1
printed by the Shenval Press London and Hertford

ACKNOWLEDGMENTS

The Author's grateful thanks are due to the following who have helped by making available drawings and photographs and who have so kindly given permission for them to be here reproduced:

The Arts Council of Great Britain
Messrs. Baker and Wilton
Ian Carter, Esq.
Messrs. Common Ground Ltd.
Walter M. Cooper, Esq.
His Grace the Duke of Devonshire, K.G.
J. Ralph Edwards, Esq., F.S.A., A.R.W.A., F.R.I.B.A.
The Enthoven Collection of the Victoria and Albert Museum
The Most Hon. The Marquess of Exeter, K.G.
Mrs. Edith L. Green
The Ipswich Central Library
The Metropolitan Museum of Art, New York
The National Buildings Record
Messrs. Penguin Books Ltd.
Henry F. Traylen, Esq., F.R.I.B.A.
R. F. Wills, Esq.
The Committee of the Wren Society

and to the Trustees of the Sir John Soane Museum by whose courtesy Plates Nos. 5, 17, 18, 19, 20, and 21 are reproduced.

CONTENTS

LIST OF ILLUSTRATIONS

The Figures in the Text

The Plates

Plates 3, 5, 6, 8, 9, 17, 18, 19, 20, 21, 24, 34, 35, 36, 38, 40, 41, 42, 45, 46, 49, 51, 52, 53, 54 and Figs. 5, 6, 7, 8, 14, 15, 20, 21, 22, 23, 24, 25, are reproduced from negatives in the collection of Common Ground Ltd.

Plates 2, 3, 4, 6, 7, 24, 39, 40, 45 appear in a film strip entitled *The English Playhouse* by Richard Southern, produced by the same firm.

Chapter One

OLD PRINTS AND BEGINNINGS

Elizabethan Sources—Wren's Drury Lane, 1674
The Royalty Theatre, Wellclose Square, 1787

THE GEORGIAN PLAYHOUSE was the British solution to a problem which had been rising in Europe for more than a century—the problem of framing the new form of theatrical presentation that sprang out of the Renaissance.

The two main novelties of the Renaissance theatre-show were, first, painted scenery of a special form and, second, an emphasis on spectacular and operatic style rather than on direct dialogue. In England the Stuart court masques under Inigo Jones were the type of the new form, and these were private entertainments—the public theatre used little painted scenery and maintained the Elizabethan style of drama. But at the Restoration, the masque type of presentation was introduced to the public and a new form of playhouse was needed to house it and to set off its new and gorgeous effects to best advantage.

In England, the old tradition of popular drama was unusually rich, and the new Restoration playhouse had to provide for both types of show—the dramatic and the operatic. Indeed, a special third type of show might almost be distinguished as well where both streams were combined—the dramatic opera. Hence it is not surprising that the playhouse in England began with unusual features, since it, above all others in Europe, had to serve two traditions—the new one of the scenic show, demanding a special auditorium in which to sit and watch, and the old one of Elizabethan dramatic form, making special demands for short, quickly-changing scenes of dialogue with many and diversified entrances and appearances.

The playhouse at the opening of the Georgian period was, then, something comparatively new, something which had existed only for about fifty years, and was still in the experimental stage of development. By the time the Georgian period was over, however, the whole form of the British theatre-building had been settled into a tradition, and there had spread throughout the kingdom a neat, logical pattern of playhouse, very typical of the genius of the age but differing markedly from anything to be seen on the Continent.

The Georgian playhouse was not only a landmark in the history of theatre design, but it was also a national creation of a decidedly individual pattern.

The Restoration and Elizabethan contributions to this final Georgian form must open our study.

The first theatre which can claim to be the direct ancestor of ours today was opened by Sir William Davenant in 1661 at the Restoration of King Charles II. It was The Duke's Theatre, Lincoln's Inn Fields. It had a roof, it used full scenery with wings, back scenes and borders, it had boxes, pit and galleries, and in that part of the theatre between the stage and auditorium—the part today that we call the proscenium arch—it had some highly interesting and individual features.

It was a novelty. The theatres before that time had not been quite like this. The Elizabethan playhouses had mostly no roof over the central part, and those few 'private' theatres which were roofed did not regularly use scenery—which was indeed a luxury rarely to be seen anywhere but at Court. But the public Elizabethan playhouses of the open type had certain features which were highly necessary to the presentation of the drama of the times, and which were indispensable, in some form, to the novel and ambitious new theatres of the Restoration which were to be the ancestors of our own. Let us then consider these indispensable parts of the Elizabethan playhouse.

Only five contemporary drawings are known to exist of the

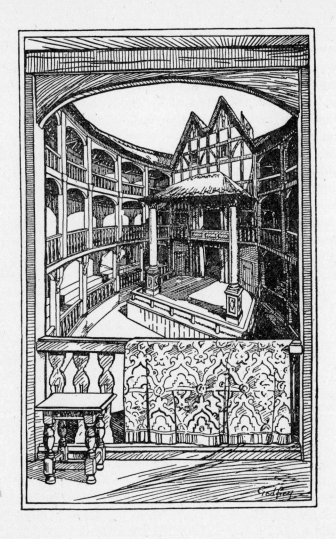

Fig. 1: An Elizabethan Playhouse interior. A reconstruction by Walter H. Godfrey, F.S.A., F.R.I.B.A.   [*By courtesy of Penguin Books*

B

interior of theatres of this period and none gives us a complete picture of what present research suggests the playhouse looked like. We must then fall back upon reconstruction. If we were to imagine ourselves looking out across the central yard from one of the galleries[1] we should notice how the surrounding auditorium embraced the sides of the stage; the players would perform *in* the auditorium, not, as ours do, *before* it.

Next we should see that in order to enter on this 'peninsular' stage, the players had to use *doors* at the back on either side. So much did entrance through a door become part of the tradition of acting that doors were built as a regular feature upon the Georgian stage, and the actors for well over a century used these doors for their entrances and exits instead of—save on rare occasions—coming on through the scenery.

Between the doors, the back wall of the Elizabethan stage was pierced with an opening. In the opening was a traverse curtain. Upon this *inner stage* certain special scenes were played, and here there might have been used on occasion certain 'scenic properties' or pieces of furniture and decoration essential to the character of the piece. These could be concealed at the closing of the curtain and changed for a later scene. Apart from this no curtain was used on the stage; the first player's entrance opened a scene and the last player's exit closed it. In spite of this lack of full scenery it must not be forgotten that such playhouses were brightly and skilfully painted and the stages colourfully and possibly elaborately decorated. The idea of a bare, crude stage is no longer supported.

Above the doors were two side *balconies* whence those frequent and refreshing scenes on two levels, which diversified the drama of the time, were played. Between them, over the central opening, was a further balcony frequently used by the musicians. So popular were these scenes between a player on the stage and one 'up aloft' that we

[1] See Fig. 1.

find all through the Restoration drama, and into the Georgian, frequent examples of scenes from windows and balconies, which, though they were manifestly the windows and balconies of the building referred to in the scenery, yet were usually played in openings built into the proscenium which was, equally manifestly, part of the auditorium.

In the Restoration period all these features were maintained in the new form of playhouse, but arranged in new positions to accord with three notable innovations. These innovations were a completely roofed theatre, an auditorium designed in artificial perspective, and—upon the stage—full and elaborate scenery capable of changing totally as required.

For a matter of eighty years or so after 1661 there was some uncertainty and experiment in the adjustment of the parts, then followed the Georgian era proper which saw the ordered fruition of the style. A useful introduction to the stages of experiment and development may be had from the history of the Father of all English theatres—Drury Lane—which set the pattern in its alterations and reconstructions for all the theatres in the land.

The Drury Lane of which we have the earliest record was not the first but the fourth of the Restoration theatres. Of the preceding three—The Duke's, Lincoln's Inn Fields (1661); The Theatre Royal, Bridges Street (1663); and the Duke's Theatre, Dorset Garden (1671)—we have no informative picture (except in the case of the latter, two exteriors and five scenes on the stage showing part of the proscenium, first printed as illustrations to Elkanah Settle's *The Empress of Morocco* in 1673 and frequently reproduced since).

The first considerable record of a playhouse-interior is a sectional drawing by the architect, Sir Christopher Wren[1]. There is no inscription upon the drawing save the faint words 'Play House', and the identification of the design as that for the Drury Lane of 1674 is

[1] See Plate 2.

based on the correspondence of its measurements with those recorded elsewhere in a description of that theatre. Further, if the ascription is (as seems likely) correct, we still do not know if this is more than a project, nor how closely the finished building maintained this character. However that may be, some matters of first importance about the Restoration theatre can be seen in the drawing.

First and foremost is its size. The building shown is comparatively small. From the stage to the back of the auditorium is only 36 feet. There are but ten rows of seats in the pit and four in each gallery. Such a theatre could scarcely have held more than 500. Yet it was the leading playhouse of its time.

This first characteristic of the English playhouse—its smallness—is significant. As late as 1813 we find Benjamin Wyatt, in his *Observations on the Design for the Theatre Royal, Drury Lane,* saying that he was 'aware of the existence of a very popular notion, that our Theatres ought to be *very small*'—and the italics are his own. This intimacy of the English theatre arose from the persistence of the native drama. On the Continent, since the emphasis was upon opera, theatres were accordingly constructed upon a much larger scale and for a more spectacular type of presentation. In England, the magnificent legacy of the Elizabethan dramatists together with the native taste for quick action and close, vivid characterization led to a more concentrated show with great importance attached to spoken dialogue and to the humanity of the characters. Such a drama as the British produced is lost in a great auditorium. It demands to be seen near to and in detail. Thus, it is significant that in early-Georgian London, where five regular or irregular playhouses might be counted, there was yet only one specific opera house, Vanbrugh's building in the Haymarket—which never happily settled down into a satisfactory English theatre.

A further point followed: the Georgian playhouse developed an entirely different system of stage machinery from the Continental.

Abroad, great size was demanded and a great depth of cellar below the stage for sinking high scenery in scene-changes, but in England the usual scenes were designed to open in the middle and slide apart sideways, and thus little depth was needed under the stage. Furthermore, it is of first importance to understand that this opening and closing of the scenery by sliding *always took place under the eyes of the audience* and was part of the excitement and spectacle of the swiftly-moving show. Such a system was, of course, eminently suited to the typical English type of drama with many short and varied scenes as against the Continental ideal of a play with the action confined to one spot. So intimately was the system of visible scene-change a part of the British tradition that we find the actors frequently did not leave the stage at the end of the scene when the occasion demanded no more than their moving from one place to another; instead, the scene itself left the stage and the next replaced it, and the players continued straight on with their action.

To enable such a *sliding* of scenery to take place, all the pieces of a setting were supported in horizontal *grooves*, in which the edges ran like the lid of a pencil-box. This method was almost unknown outside the British stage, but it persisted here from the very beginning up to Irving's time. It is now all but forgotten. In a corner of the loft of the Theatre Royal, Bristol, however, there was discovered a few years ago, by the present writer, a fragment of one of these grooves, once part of a full set and now, so far as is known, the only survivor of this Georgian system of scene-change left in existence[1].

Something of this scenic arrangement is seen on the stage of the Wren playhouse. There are visible four wings and, behind, a set of three back scenes close together.

The drawing exemplifies one of the three notable innovations in the Georgian playhouse—the scenery. Of the other two, the roof is

[1] See Plate 1. Some explanation of the working of such grooves will be found in the study of Plymouth Theatre Royal on page 59.

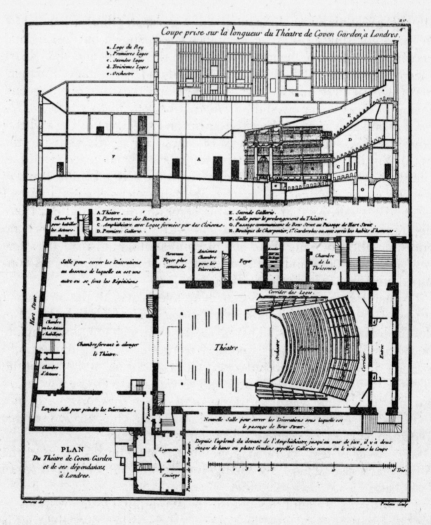

Fig. 2: Covent Garden of 1732. From a little-known French engraving of G. P. M. Dumont's (1763) reproducing the layout of Shepherd's Covent Garden   [*From 'Parallèle de plans des salles . . .' 1763*

[22]

plain to see, but the last—the trick of building the auditorium in perspective—is worth a word.

It will be noticed that the upper cornice slopes down to the proscenium, and the base of the lower boxes slopes up. This character of converging upon the stage also marked the lines of the ground plan of the auditorium. If we look at Shepherd's plans for Covent Garden[1] which, though they were made as late as 1732, are still, in feeling, a footnote to the Restoration style rather than a true example of the Georgian, we notice a feature of the English auditorium often remarked on by foreign visitors—the fan-shaped pit. This building then, although much bigger than Wren's Drury Lane, resembles it in the converging lines of its plan arising from artificial perspective. Incidentally, this is probably the earliest ground plan we have of an authentic English playhouse as distinct from an opera house.

Like Covent Garden, Wren's Drury Lane shows a heavy and elaborate column-treatment of the stage boxes and the whole proscenium unit—and in Wren's design the columns are even carried along the sides of the house as well, but it was probably soon found that such wide divisions between the boxes greatly reduced the number of spectators and the feature was, as we shall see, done away with.

In the elaboration of the proscenium sides the chief element that springs to notice is the 'doors of entrance'—those legacies from Elizabeth's day. We see there were two a side (and we can find that in some theatres there appear to have been no less than three). The acting-conventions attaching to those doors are of the greatest interest. For instance, we discover from Sir Samuel Tuke's *The Adventures of Five Hours*, produced at the Duke's Theatre, Lincoln's Inn Fields, in 1663, that two neighbouring doors could be used as a sort of substitute for scene-changing, for when in Act V, Scene 3, Antonio and Octavio are forced, fighting, off the stage by Don Henrique and his men, they retire through one door only to enter immediately by

[1] See Fig. 2.

[23]

the next, which Antonio straightway bolts, saying to his friend, 'Now we shall have a breathing while at least, Octavio, and time to look about us'; he then immediately adds—seeing, of course, that the other door by which they had just retired is cheek by jowl with that they have entered and was obviously not secured when they went through —'Pray see yon other door be fast.' And the stage direction follows: 'Octavio *steps to the door where they went out.*' No sooner has he done so than, to keep up the urgency of the chase, 'Henrique *bounces at the door they came in at.*'

So they are now in another room, but there is no indication whatever that the scenery was changed at all. Notice the vivid impression of speed and urgency arising from such a convention—a quality no Continental theatre could achieve in quite the same way, since proscenium doors were practically unknown abroad.

A fascinating study may be made of the Restoration proscenium door, and fascinating it is to stand, as we shall do later, in the last remaining Georgian proscenium doorway in England and review the great and significant effect upon the audience which the entrance of the player *in the theatre* and not *in the scenery* must once have had.

Above the doors in Wren's section may be seen the proscenium balconies—equally general and equally ingeniously used. Next to these and continuing them exactly in pattern—so linking the action of the play with the spectator in the playhouse—are the side boxes of the auditorium. These boxes became a special feature of the Georgian playhouse, and grew to encircle the whole auditorium, but in Restoration days they generally occupied only the sides of the house; the end facing the stage was occupied by tiers containing rows of open benches. The floor of the house was occupied by the last division of the Restoration auditorium—the pit, fitted with backless, green-baize-covered benches.

In following the changes by which Wren's Restoration Drury Lane grew into a leading Georgian playhouse, we find many alterations taking place during its early, formative years, but the next picture comes in 1775, when the Adam Brothers redesigned the auditorium and published a print of the scheme[1]. Wren's pilasters were dispensed with in the interests presumably of increased seating and his circles were supported on slender columns. His forestage had already been made shallower, his proscenium doors reduced to one a side, his galleries were deepened, and it would appear that his perspective convergence of building lines was straightened.

But his pit entrance is still in the same place. This is part of the fundamental structure of the building, giving as it does upon the pit passage in the basement—a highly typical feature of the early playhouse, which formed the only means of access from the front of the house to the pit, passing under the side boxes.

The Adam decorations were 'all put out by painting over them' by Thomas Greenwood, senior, and William Capon in 1783. The phrase is instructive since it shows that the Adam decorations were flat and not modelled, as a superficial glance at their print might have suggested. (It is interesting to note in this connection that George Saunders wrote concerning auditorium-decoration in *A Treatise on Theatres* in 1790—that 'No carved work, projecting ornaments, modillions, dentils, etc., of any kind should have place; the painter may here exert his talents.') Notes in Capon's hand on the new scheme[2] hint at the colour and so give us the first intimation of the traditional decoration of a Georgian playhouse; Capon says 'The ground of this new painting was a very faint kind of pea green or rather a greenish colour, the ornaments [three words struck out which appear to be *to imitate relief*, and above is substituted *chiaro scuro*]. The boxes were lined with a red or colour between pink and crimson.'

In 1792 Wren's shell was pulled down to make way for a larger house. The first phase of the Georgian era had passed and the shift to the Regency had begun, in which there was to come a new movement

[1] See Plate 3.   [2] The scheme is illustrated in Plate 4.

for bigger theatres. As we pass we should note that the development from early beginnings to the height of the Georgian style, that we shall discuss in detail in other examples, is here epitomized in the history of one house as a sort of introduction to our study.

There followed on the site of Drury Lane an immense new building by Henry Holland, one of the largest theatres in English history, but ill-fated and ill-suited to the player. In 1809 it was burnt to the ground to be replaced by Wyatt's building in 1812 which, though altered internally, stands to this day. Holland's short-lived auditorium well illustrated the immense development of the playhouse in Regency times. It contained no less than five tiers rising from a proportionately large pit, and it attempted, at first, to dispense with proscenium doors, but their day was not yet over, and soon they were reinstated in the new building[1].

A further note on the development of a single theatre is offered in the prints of the Royalty Theatre in Wellclose Square, near the Tower of London. Here was a typical building of essentially Georgian restraint and style, free from the uncertain elaboration of the earlier Restoration and guiltless as yet of the trimmings of the late Regency, apt in all its parts as an example of an ordinary Georgian theatre[2]. It was begun in 1785. The auditorium was painted stone-colour with gilding, and had crimson in the boxes. The same house was completely transformed in decoration to suit Regency taste in 1815[3].

It is interesting to compare with the known prints of this theatre a set of four architect's plans now in the Enthoven Collection. They are ascribed to Cornelius Dixon and are said to be those for the Royalty, but they are oddly inconsistent with the very clear pictures

---

[1] Plate 5 shows a hitherto unpublished sectional drawing of the auditorium which it is of considerable interest to compare with the well-known print by Rowlandson and Pugin in *The Microcosm of London*.

[2] See Plates 6 and 7.　　[3] See Plates 8 and 9.

we possess of the house as it actually appeared. The plans[1], only one of which has been published before, form however an interesting example of a period of Georgian theatre construction which is unfortunately too rare in our records. They include a specimen of the layout of the basement walls under the auditorium of the period which is especially worth study as being possibly the only information of the sort available to us, and it may be usefully compared with the evidence gained from the study of the pit passages at Bristol and at Richmond, Surrey, and—most notably—at Richmond, Yorkshire.

[1] See Plates 10, 11, 12 and 13.

Chapter Two

GEORGIAN TOWN THEATRES

Bath, 1750 and 1805—Limerick, 1788
Richmond, Surrey, 1765—Bristol, 1766

GEORGIAN THEATRES ARE rare in Britain today, and the few that remain are generally in poor preservation or have been altered, or even cleared of all theatrical details, at a later date. All the same we have, now, in order to obtain the fullest picture, to compare such surviving buildings with the remainder of the evidence in prints, and in this chapter we turn to actual buildings.

In London no Georgian theatre remains. The first theatres to be built outside London were naturally in the larger and more fashionable towns. It is not surprising then that the earliest provincial theatres of which we have actual remains are town theatres. They, then, form the subject of this chapter.

Many booths and small experimental playhouses were used in the early eighteenth century but it was about the fifties and sixties that the town theatre really came into its own in England. The movement spread and by the eighties country playhouses were to be found even in small market towns, and some of these are discussed in the next chapter.

Probably the oldest building of its sort left to us is that which once housed the Theatre Royal, Orchard Street, Bath. It was opened in 1750 and closed in 1805, after which the interior—today a Freemasons' hall—was entirely altered, but the shell remains substantially as it was.

The exterior in Orchard Street was plain[1] and the present pedi-

[1] See Plate 14.

mented entrance is later work. The original trio of doors to boxes, pit and gallery were once side by side where now three windows are to be seen.

The vanished interior was recorded by a water-colourist named Nixon. The whereabouts of his painting is now unknown to the present author, but a reproduction was published several years ago in Mowbray Green's *The Eighteenth Century Architecture of Bath*. In spite of its interest, however, as showing the only known interior view of the oldest remaining playhouse in Britain, it might yet have been omitted as a second-hand reproduction of a somewhat crude drawing but for one fact. This fact is that recent discoveries have brought to light certain other very little-known drawings of Bath theatres, and it is now possible for the first time to assemble all these and so present a picture of the development of one of the earliest Georgian playhouses from its first years, through all its alterations, right to the present time. Forming as it does a link in so interesting a chain, the Nixon water-colour takes an added value and its in- clusion here, even at second hand, is justified[1].

Briefly, the story the pictures illustrate is this: eighteen years after it was opened (that is in 1768), Palmer, the manager, obtained let- ters patent from King George III for this theatre. Only two other theatres in Britain at that time owned such a patent, namely Drury Lane and Covent Garden. Bath then became the first provincial playhouse to bear the title 'Theatre Royal'.

The water-colour of Nixon's suggests that originally there was a plain and simple auditorium, wherein the flourish of the Restoration had settled down to an early-Georgian restraint. The arrangement of the seating was typical. There was an open pit in the centre of the house with a sloping floor built to give the spectators the best view of the stage. The fact of the slope is seen by comparing the height of the heads of the spectators near the stage with the box-panels above

[1] See Plate 15 and also Plates 16 to 21 and Figs. 3 and 4.

them—the heads are well below the boxes and the pittites are flanked by a brick wall of a different colour from the box panels and forming a sort of basement to them; but the heads of the nearer spectators rise well up into these panels.

This independence of design between the pit and the rest of the house is characteristic of all Georgian theatres; the decoration of the house proper rises from the level of the stage where the lower boxes spring. Below that level is another world with which the design of the auditorium is quite unrelated. To this point we shall return.

Above this separate Georgian pit with its green-covered, backless benches rose the boxes on either side of the house. These boxes were a highly characteristic part of the Georgian theatre. There was no first circle with the pit going back underneath it as we know it today. Instead, immediately round the brink of the smaller pit sat a tier of boxes whose ledges were within handreach of the pittites below. These boxes were formed by subdividing the rows of seats with low partitions into small units each to contain about a dozen people. A box could be taken as a whole or its seats could be sold separately, but it meant that these highest-priced seats in the house were divided into small separate groups, each group attaining to some extent a sense of privacy and cosiness. Indeed, in the later part of the period the specifically *private* box arose, whose partitions were ceiling-high and which had its own door and even curtains at the front (or screens or lattices) to cut off the occupants and their devices from all but the festive atmosphere of the house if they so desired.

In Restoration days the boxes tended to be reserved to the sides of the house, while those seats at the end opposite the stage were arranged more as an open circle[1]. In the Georgian period the boxes spread right round to encircle the whole pit and to the side boxes

[1] See Plate 2 and also Plate 3 where the first signs of subdivision are visible.

were added what were (a little confusingly) called the front boxes, or those facing the stage at what we should call the back of the auditorium.

The tier above was possibly similarly divided into boxes at the side, but was nearly always developed into an open circle facing the stage[1]. In small theatres this tier might be left out.

The third, or topmost, tier was sometimes subdivided at the sides —when this part was often called the Green Boxes (possibly because they partook of the general colour of the house and were not lined with gorgeous crimson like those below)—and sometimes left undivided, when it was called the Slips. It is possible that in some theatres the slips were not even provided with seats, but formed a sort of promenade graced, maybe, with one loose bench. Sometimes the slips were entirely omitted and there was left only that portion of the topmost tier facing the stage which was, however, always open, and was the Gallery—the true home of the Gods.

Returning to the Nixon water-colour we may see how the elaborate Restoration proscenium had now become simplified, retaining scarcely any architectural trimmings, but simply keeping its essential features, the doors of entrance, limited to one a side.

Above the doors were balconies or continuations of the second tier, used, it seems, indiscriminately by players or audience according to the need of the show.

Upon his stage Nixon affords a splendid example of the easy regard in which the Georgians held scenery—a palpable landscape with trees, river and a distant castle, is quite happily framed in a set of column wings that were surely meant for a classical interior—but these were the days of Stock Scenery; it was used for its own fun not for any highfalutin purpose of giving a deceptive impression of the appearance of the place where the action was supposed to occur. And the action here—in spite of the costume—looks very much as if it

[1] See Plate 4 and also Fig. 12.

were the famous Ghost Scene from *Hamlet* itself; thus it would have been presented to the Georgians.

This Orchard Street theatre was improved and altered in 1755, again improved and reconstructed in 1767 (when the auditorium was given a dome), and, about 1775, reconstructed again (when the dome, 'injurious both to sight and hearing', was removed) by the original architect, Palmer; and what must have been—if the truth were known—an intolerably ill-ventilated, unupholstered playhouse, where drippings from the candles in the heat ruined the pittites' clothes, now settled on a career which was to take it to the new world of the following century. But its days there were numbered. The rising times demanded a better house, and in 1805 Orchard Street was abandoned and the Theatre Royal was transferred to Dance and Palmer's new building in Beauford Square, and we may there note the development of the Georgian theatre into the Regency.

The exterior again stands today and may be compared with one of George Dance's sketches. Inside, the house was arranged in the typical late-Georgian fashion with a pit and three tiers. The ceiling still maintains the traditional slant, but the lines of the tiers below are horizontal, consequently the bronzed cast-iron columns supporting the ceiling from the upper tier are graduated in height and lead, at the end of the house facing the stage, to a pleasant conceit of rising arches which—at any rate in one stage of the project—were interpreted as a screen of slender palm-trees. The front row of seats in each tier projected in front of the supporting columns and so allowed the occupants to have a clear view of the stage and offered some foreshadowing of the later balcony.

The proscenium feature was elegantly and very simply treated, with the doors in a curve, and a sort of shell-niche surmounting the upper of the two small balconies. The ceiling scheme was specially designed to incorporate a set of five paintings by Cassali, once in Beckford's mansion at Fonthill.

Fig. 3 (*above*): Interior of Dance's Theatre, Beauford Square, Bath, built 1805
Fig. 4 (*below*): Interior of Phipps' Theatre, Beauford Square, Bath, built 1863

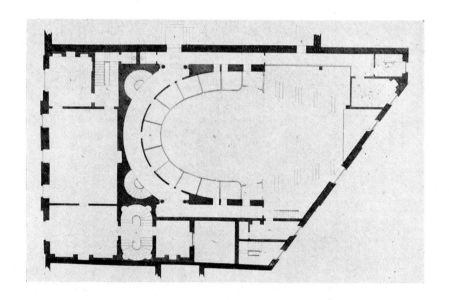

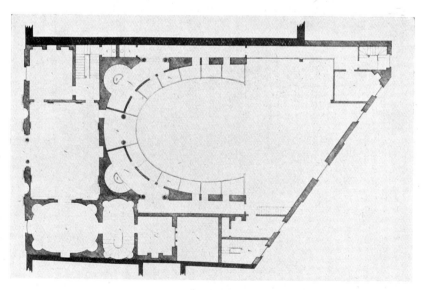

Fig. 5 (*above*): Ground Floor Plan of James Lewis's Theatre at Limerick, 1788
Fig. 6 (*below*): Plan of 'One Pair Floor' of Limerick Theatre

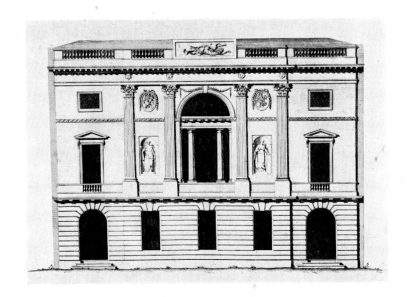

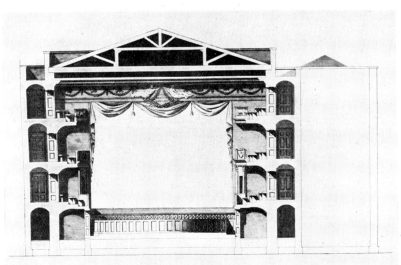

Fig. 7 (*above*): Façade of Limerick Theatre
Fig. 8 (*below*): Cross section through auditorium of Limerick Theatre
⎡*From James Lewis's 'Original Designs in Architecture'*

Fig. 9: The Actor on the Forestage. This print is given to illustrate the close relation between an actor on the Georgian fore-stage and his audience—at
least those members in the nearer boxes, although this sense of intimacy
was probably communicated to the whole house. Note the proscenium
door, and the lower stage box only seen in bigger theatres

[*Richard Southern Collection*

The scheme for the theatre as a whole seems to have been the work of various hands, for we find that it was erected under the direction of Palmer, the city architect, while George Dance is only mentioned as 'responsible for the ornamental parts of the building, and especially the "grand front".' This combination of hands in the scheme is perhaps responsible for certain tentative notes on Dance's plans such as 'The intended floor of the pit', 'Supposed line of the ceiling', 'This floor (or beam) is in place', which otherwise suggest an oddly undecided plan.

A print of 1824 shows this building with its Cassali ceiling, in a blaze of glory on the occasion of His Majesty King George IV's birthday, when a Royal Dramatic Fête was held. It is especially interesting in giving an example of the old custom of flooring-in the pit on special occasions to provide a great unbroken surface, level with the stage, so creating an assembly- or ball-room. Herein may be seen one of the reasons for designing the Georgian auditorium so that its decorative scheme started from the base of the lower boxes and was independent of the pit. When the pit was covered the effect of the house was still a unity.

Dance's interior was gutted by fire in 1862 and rebuilt by Phipps the following year. Here again we may form an impression of the development of auditorium design in Mid-Victorian days from an existing print of the building. Now the Georgian circle of boxes is much modified and the proscenium doors are gone. The link with the auditorium of today is seen to be almost complete. There remained one essential anachronism—the intrusive columns supporting the circles, which modern advance in construction has taught us to avoid, but which were almost indispensable characteristics of the Georgian playhouse.

We say 'almost' because a recent discovery suggests that in his designs for a theatre at Limerick, James Lewis had anticipated this improvement. Although columns were not avoided in London till at

Fig. 10: Theatre at Richmond, Surrey, opened 1765. The stage

[Richard Southern Collection

the earliest the 1860s, it would appear that Lewis produced at Limerick as early as 1788 a neat little auditorium with no columns at all—at any rate no sign of them is to be found on his plans. If this is indeed so, he produced a playhouse which was three-quarters of a century ahead of its times.

Fifteen years after Orchard Street, Bath, was opened, that is in 1765, another theatre was built near a city and, though now totally destroyed, it left a few late records which fit well into our story and provide valuable information.

The theatre was on the Green at Richmond, Surrey. It was a tiny house but it possessed a pair of proscenium doors and a creditable tier of Georgian boxes round the little pit, together with upper side

Fig. 11: Theatre at Richmond, Surrey. The stage

boxes and a gallery facing the stage—an epitome of the smaller Georgian auditorium.

Certain drawings made at the time of the theatre's demolition in 1884 include some information on a very rarely illustrated part of the Georgian playhouse, information which is unavailable in other than pictorial form and of which the proper understanding leads to one of the most important discoveries about the chief of all Georgian theatre relics—the playhouse at the other Richmond, in Yorkshire. This rarely illustrated element is the pit passage—the subterranean access which we have already imagined lying behind the pit door in Wren's drawing for Drury Lane and in the Adams' reconstruction[1]. The passage here shown leads from a stair-foot in the front of the house, runs under the side boxes on the spectator's right of the

[1] See Fig. 13 and compare with Plates 2 and 3.

Figs. 12 and 13: Theatre at Richmond, Surrey
(*above*) The auditorium. (*below*) The pit passage   [*Richard Southern Collection*

auditorium, and has at its far end a door barring the public from the fascinating region under the stage (to visit which we must wait till our introduction to Bristol). Turning off from this passage to the left, just before the door to the under-stage machine room, is the entrance to the front or deepest part of the pit, the floor of which would be reached up two or three steps[1]. By this small passage (a death trap to modern fire authorities) the Georgian playgoer had his only access to the pit.

How this drawing illuminates our understanding of the theatre at Richmond, Yorkshire, will be seen in the next chapter.

The Theatre Royal, Bristol, is the earliest existing British theatre retaining anything of a Georgian interior. It was opened in 1766 and still stands today after a hundred and eighty years of theatrical life. It has suffered frequent alteration and modernization, but sufficient of the original form remains to illustrate the town theatre at the apogee of the Georgian era.

One of the first interests to the student is that the Theatre Royal, Bristol, appears to have been a very close replica of the Drury Lane of its time. Since that time was the year 1766, the then Drury Lane would have been the Wren building of 1674 after it had undergone its earlier developments but before its remodelling by the Adams. One can then take the present theatre at Bristol to reflect something of those early modifications on Wren's Restoration plan which kept his theatre up to the taste of the times as it grew into the Georgian age.

A longitudinal section through the Bristol theatre together with plans at the pit level and at that of the middle boxes were among the drawings made in 1942 by J. Ralph Edwards, F.R.I.B.A., before the recent renovation. It is interesting to place the section of the auditorium beside that of Wren's auditorium reproduced to the same

[1] An example of these steps may be seen in Fig. 15.

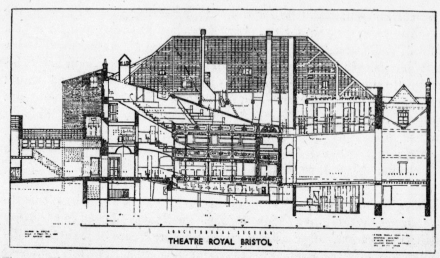

LONGITUDINAL SECTION
THEATRE ROYAL BRISTOL

Fig. 14: Theatre Royal, Bristol. Longitudinal section through theatre. Drawn by
J. Ralph Edwards, F.R.I.B.A.

scale[1]. We find the length of the houses practically the same. We
notice a considerable difference in the Bristol gallery, but we learn
with interest that this gallery was added some years after the theatre
was built. We see a much shallower forestage at Bristol, but we discover that Wren's forestage was cut down about 1696 and his proscenium doors reduced to one a side, the lower being replaced by a
box. Moreover, we find signs that the forestage at Bristol, now
practically non-existent, originally ran forward to the foot of the
farther box-pilaster[2]. We see something of the same perspective
slanting of the lines of the boxes in Bristol as at Drury Lane, and,
finally, but with special interest, we note great Corinthian pilasters
at Bristol like those of Wren's theatre *but now reduced to only two*

[1] See Plate 24.

[2] See Plate 23, which photograph was specially taken for comparison with the
Wren design in Plate 2.

[38]

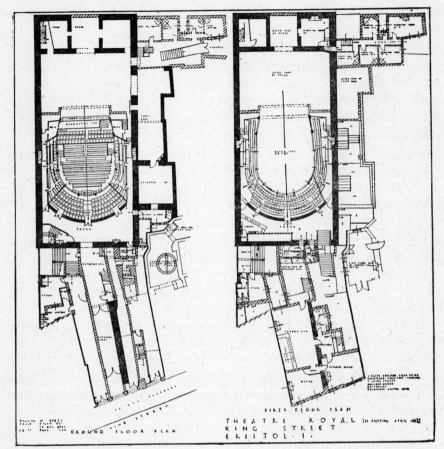

Fig. 15: Theatre Royal, Bristol. Plans at pit and first-floor levels. Drawn by J. Ralph Edwards, F.R.I.B.A.

flanking the stage box. The remainder of the tiers are supported on slender, typically Georgian columns. Thus it may be that the great pilasters fronting Wren's boxes were already partially removed by 1766 and replaced by smaller columns similar to those in the Adams'

[39]

design of 1775—or it may be that originally Bristol had similar great pilasters and altered them to the present columns at a later date (John Summerson claims that the reeded columns now at Bristol are rarely found as early as 1766). But the chief fact remains that the two buildings are very close in size and fundamental arrangement and that probably no closer impression of Garrick's auditorium at Drury Lane can ever now be had than that given by this theatre at Bristol, which we today should class as small[1].

In examining the detail at Bristol great care must be exercised. The box-front decorations are all superposed Victorian plaster-work. The vaunted proscenium doors cannot be original and have modern plywood in their surround.

The boxes in the lower tier no longer have their Georgian partitions, but a careful examination of the posts at the back of the seats[2] will disclose signs of the old housing of such partitions, and of the shape of the rail or capping-mould which crowned the tops. Below on the floor under the present seats are to be found still further remnants.

It is to be hoped that in the near future some of the Victorian ornaments may be stripped from the box-fronts, for there are clear signs that underneath all the florid plasterwork is simple Georgian panelling. For instance, when one of the women's heads was recently removed there were disclosed underneath gilded triglyphs and guttae of classic Georgian style upon a traditional green-painted ground[3].

The ceiling is a superb piece of work, carried out in gilded

---

[1] The comparison may further be made of Plate 3, showing the Adam alterations to the Wren building, with Plate 22 which was photographed especially from a viewpoint as nearly as possible corresponding to that of the Adam print.

[2] See for instance near the right-hand edge of Plate 25.

[3] Such Heads are visible above the columns in Plate 23 and the Georgian work revealed underneath is seen in Plate 26.

modelling upon a rich moss green[1], forming a glittering and romantic 'sky' to a shadowy auditorium gleaming in candlelight. But here again, especially over the one-time forestage, are signs of alterations to the original scheme.

Supremely well exemplified at Bristol is the pit passage[2] such as we saw among the illustrations of Richmond, Surrey, with, facing the actual opening into the pit, a niche in the thickness of the outside wall. Just as before, the passage ends in a 'private' door barring the path to the understage world.

Were we to open this door we should find ourselves in a forest of machinery[3]. Before us, projecting from above, are lever-handles which once opened 'cuts' in the stage through which scenery used to rise, and bevies of fairies be lifted in charming poses on the great 'bridges' or rising platforms visible in the middle distance. To the right is the smaller platform of a 'corner trap', behind it again a 'grave trap', and in the well beneath all this profusion are the great drums and shafts which lent power to the working ropes actuating the complex machinery.

Much of the fabric here is possibly no older than Victorian, but few theatres in England can boast so complete a set of old stage machinery. We hope that it may never now suffer modernization, but remain a unique museum of old glories.

Above on the stage itself we note at the back a relic of the 'inner stage'[4], which can be seen in Wren's section in a slightly different form, and which was ultimately derived from the Elizabethan inner stage. Its use in Georgian times was to provide extra depth when, on the occasions of special spectacular set scenes, a deep vista was needed for effects or processions.

The fascination of this theatre extends to the loft above the auditorium ceiling. Here among the timbers of the roof may still be seen the double sloping trough down which great spherical iron weights

[1] See Plate 27.   [2] See Plate 28.   [3] See Plate 30.   [4] See Plate 29.

were rolled, which not only gave the pealing of thunder, but communicated its reverberations to the very fabric of the house itself—and sounded, as thunder should, not from back stage but from above the hearers' heads[1].

[1] See Plate 31.

Chapter Three

GEORGIAN COUNTRY THEATRES

Stamford, 1768—Richmond, Yorkshire, 1788—Newbury, 1802

A s THE GEORGIAN period develops we find, as we anticipated, a growth of little theatres in the country—or at least in quite small towns. Of these the gem is at Richmond in Yorkshire, but a building at Stamford, Lincolnshire, claims our attention first as only two years later than Bristol.

Stamford is one of the most perfect Georgian towns in England and to hear that it possesses a theatre dating from 1768 is a call to any investigator. But there is a mournful qualification.

Mr. J. Clare Billing, a local historian, informs us that 'The whole of the interior fittings, proscenium, curtains, scenery, stalls, etc., were sold in 1871.' Since this happened to so many of our Georgian theatres, it is not uninteresting to pause for a moment and realize just what is meant. The extent of such a sale and its effect in removing any significant character from a theatre may be gathered from a faded manuscript in the Plymouth Municipal Records relating to just such a sale of the interior of the little Frankfort Gate Theatre of that city, built in or about 1758. We read—'The articles to be disposed of either at a valuation, or included in the price for the premises, fixtures, etc., are—the scenery and all the beams to which it is attached from the front of the Proscenium to the back wall of the stage. . . . All the Frames and machinery of whatever description for working the scenery both above and below the stage—the Pit, box and gallery seats—The Orchestra Partition—all interior doors except those of the dressing room—The Fronts of the boxes and gallery—The Stage floor and all beams thereto attached not necessary to support the

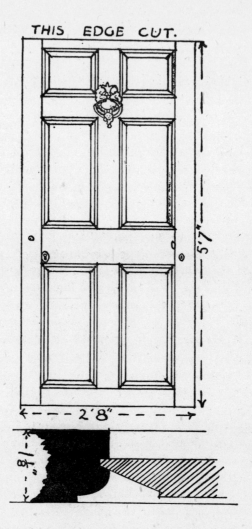

Fig. 16: Stamford Theatre, Lincs. Drawing of presumed proscenium door discovered in the cellar in 1946. Measured by H. F. Traylen, F.R.I.B.A.

building—the back partition of the boxes. The Proscenium and all Theatric scenery from the back wall to the orchestra and other parts of the premises.' And so there would be little left to give a hint to an historian. Thus it happened at Stamford, and neither the hall nor the loft above provide any significant trace of theatrical details.

There remain, however, the façade[1] and the cellar. In the latter are many walls and rooms of various dates still needing close study, with one feature at least that may have a direct theatrical significance. At the foot of a short twisting stair near the centre of the building there still stands a door which is clearly out of place. It is of Georgian proportion and bears a pleasant ring-shaped knocker, and what appear to be traces of gilding on the mouldings. The door is of too light a structure, it would seem, ever to have served as a street door, and the possibility arises that it was once one of the two proscenium doors of the old theatre. If that can be proved it becomes a relic of high interest and may claim to be the only remaining example at present known[2].

Now that the war-uses of this hall as a soldiers' club are over, it might well be that a return to its original purpose could be considered, and today knowledge of the small Georgian auditorium of the country town is growing sufficiently for a restoration—or at least a reconstruction upon authentic lines—to be not impossible. The result might offer not only a museum-exhibit of a very high interest—according well with the character and traditions of the town and with the pleasant dignity of the façade—but a civic meeting-place for the resumption of the theatrical life of Stamford which has too long been missing. Its details might be closely based on those of the next playhouse we turn to study.

[1] See Plate 32.

[2] Its details are to be seen in Fig. 16 and Plate 33.

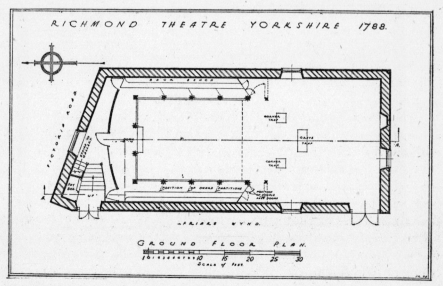

Fig. 17: Theatre at Richmond, Yorkshire. Plan drawn by J. Ravens

The exterior of the little building which holds the theatre of Richmond, Yorkshire, is perhaps the plainest in our whole survey. The house is of local stone with a simple pitch-roof and—except for one slightly diagonal end-wall to accord with the shape of the site—is an unrelieved rectangle[1]. It stands at the junction of Victoria Road with Friars Wynd. The end wall facing Victoria Road looks north and contains, at the top, a small, louvered ventilator to the loft above the gallery ceiling, then, below, the window to the gallery, next that to the vestibule, and, last, a low, squarish door at street level to the cellar. Just round the corner, in Friars Wynd, is the entrance door, and from this north end to the south the ground slopes sharply up.

Since one's experience in passing through this entrance door to visit the auditorium is probably closer to that of the original Geor-

[1] See Plate 34 and Fig. 17.

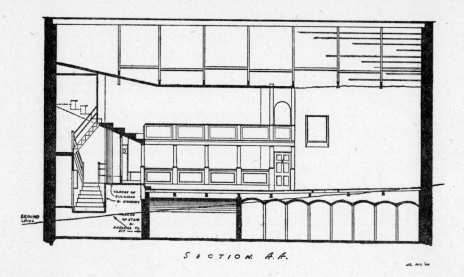

SECTION A.A.

Fig. 18: Theatre at Richmond, Yorkshire. Section drawn by J. Ravens

gian playgoer than may be gained in any other place in the land, we may usefully describe it in detail.

Within the door is a tiny stone-flagged floor with steps beyond up to the vestibule level[1]. To the right of these steps, the wall is slightly broken forward at the second riser. This nearer portion, as we shall see, is the walled-up entrance to a cellar passage. To the left, on the opposite side of the steps, is the paybox[2]. The flight of seven steps carries us up to the vestibule level whence stairs lead to the gallery. This vestibule reaches completely across the end of the building and contains, in its right-hand wall, three doors giving on to the boxes[3]. Passing through the centre of these we enter the auditorium and walk through towards the stage and turn to survey the theatre. Some dozen years ago the prospect would not have been

[1] See Plate 35.   [2] See Plate 36.   [3] See Plate 38.

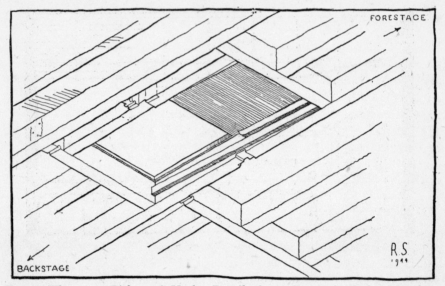

Fig. 19: Theatre at Richmond, Yorks. Detail of trap. Drawn by Richard Southern

immediately promising[1]. Cleansing and much study were needed to recognize the significance of the place.

The chief impression when the effect of disrepair was cleared away might be found disappointing. Some essential of a theatre was missing. One sees that the floor is continuous throughout the building, consequently there appears no raised stage. Further, a local rumour—perpetuated in the *Sunday Times* of July 25th, 1943— asserted that this theatre never had a stage but that the players always performed on the same level as the audience. If, moreover, one leaves the auditorium and visits the basement below one finds a solidly-built vaulted wine-cellar, whose crown is within a few inches of the floor above, and which extends under the whole theatre except the vestibule. The cellar seems as solid as the foundations,

[1] See Plate 39.

and the flat lifeless floor of the theatre seems to have existed since the place was built.

But in 1788, when Samuel Butler begged leave to erect this house, his letter to the Mayor and Corporation intimated that he would 'with their approval and assistance erect a proper Theatre'. Now a 'proper Theatre' to an English man-of-the-stage in 1788 was a building equipped with all the theatrical features we have so far noted in this study of the Georgian playhouse, and those included a stage furnished with machinery, and an auditorium with all the traditional features of sunk pit, encircling boxes and gallery above. So firmly had the tradition of the arrangement of the Georgian auditorium been fixed by this time that to understand the main features of one is to have a guide to the layout of all. This was not a period of ambitious innovations or experiments, and a 'proper' theatre meant then a theatre true to type.

It was, therefore, no surprise to the writer to discover, on raising the floor-boards at a part of the stage where tradition had established that a trap-door would be situated, that under the square opening, the arrangement of the floor joists was such as to form an oblong framing, and that on the side faces of the two longer joists flanking this opening there was arranged a sloping groove.

There could be only one use for this groove, namely, to allow a trap-door to drop down and slide aside to reveal the opening. Such an opening is useless if it communicates with no lower region. Therefore there must once have been a clear space under here and one deep enough for the working of the rising platform of a trap and for its machinery. Therefore, again, the present vaulted brick cellar under the theatre is a later addition, and hence the present lack of any sunk pit in the auditorium is the result of later alterations, and the original character of the house in this respect was quite different.

Study of the building in this new light confirms the above theory. Signs of the original pit entrance are to be found and it is possible to

E

trace the one-time existence of a pit-passage leading down steps from an opening opposite the pay-box referred to earlier. This passage was probably closely similar in appearance to that at Richmond, Surrey, or at Bristol. Traces also exist of the opening leading out of the passage to the pit itself, and we may ascertain the exact floorboard at which the stage ended, and confidently claim that, from this point to the back of the hall, the present floor was once occupied by a typical sloping pit. Thus Richmond, Yorkshire, becomes a 'proper' Georgian theatre embodying better than any other building yet discovered all the known characteristics of the late eighteenth-century theatre of the country-town of England, and we are in a position to reconstruct what is likely to be a very close approximation of its original appearance[1].

Now that the great interest of this building as the only remaining example, approaching perfection, of its age is established, attention has been turned to it by several national bodies, and it may be that in the near future a restoration of its pit to approximately its original form will be undertaken, and thus the chief imperfection be removed which mars its claim to be a full example of the subject of this book— the Georgian playhouse.

During the 1939 war the building was used as a paper-salvage depot. At this time a fire partially destroyed one of the proscenium sides. The door within the proscenium doorway was damaged and was unfortunately removed and broken up. Thus we lost a signally rare piece of Georgian theatre furniture (the opposite door had been removed long before), but there remains a photograph to witness the appearance of probably the last proscenium door to be seen in its place in England. Now, however, it is to be hoped that this sad

[1] See the model illustrated in Plate 40 where the nearer wall with the near-side boxes and gallery have been removed for clearness. The present entrance door is seen facing out of the bottom left-hand corner of the picture, with a glimpse of the one-time steps that led down to the pit-passage.

period of whittling-away the expressive details of the Georgian playhouse is over. We are thankful that the proscenium doorway at least remains, and the typical balcony above[1].

We have only in imagination to set the stage with scenery (we could do worse than take temporarily as our model that shown in Plate 46, although it is a century too late), and we may come nearer to bodying forth the reality of the Georgian playhouse as it was than anything but a voyage into the past itself would give. Here is our closest contact with the Georgian at the play. As audience, we may picture ourselves in these boxes (whose dwarf partitions, sloping back from each pillar, are faintly seen reconstructed in the model) and watch the player enter by the proscenium door and, almost within reach of us, deliver his soliloquy on the forestage. Or, as player— and this is the most instructive of all—we may ourselves pass this doorway and stand upon the forestage and see, and feel, about us the ancient house with its candles, and experience the power it gives to reach out and hold without the slightest effort, the attention of the audience in every corner. The sense of communication here is notable and delicate. One may well understand that the intimacy represented in contemporary caricatures is not exaggerated[2].

Since this is the only spot in Britain, and perhaps in the world, where the feeling of the contact of the Georgian actor with his audience may be revived, it is deeply to be hoped that this building and its unique character may be carefully and understandingly preserved, and, if restored, may, now and then, be used to stage a Georgian performance.

[1] The doorway and balcony and the relation of these essential parts to the stage of the time may still be studied in Plates 37, 41 and 42. In Plate 41 is the stage as seen from the gallery, so photographed that the rail across the end of the gallery cuts out vision of the floor of the house just at the point where the old stage finished. In Plate 42 this line between stage and pit is marked by laying a black cloth over all that part of the floor which was once sunk pit.

[2] See Fig. 9.

For a footnote to our chapter on the 'country' theatre of the Georgians, we go to Newbury in Berkshire. With Newbury the reading of the old and faded parchment of the past becomes hard indeed. Had we not already the evidence of earlier buildings to inform our interpretation we could make but little of this chilly furniture store in Speenhamland, that was earlier a cow-shed, and once a Georgian playhouse. But for all that, given the knowledge to be had from Richmond and Bristol, we can see in the little shell enough to understand how it, too, might have touched a former glory and had the candles glittering upon its boxes at some visiting night of Kemble's or of Kean's.

The building, which is said to have been opened in 1802, after an earlier building in Northcroft Lane, offers on one special point a warning to investigators. It exists today in a sad state of disrepair, presenting a forlorn four walls and a roof; one might be inclined to dismiss it as showing no trace at all of the vestibules and entrances which are essential to a playhouse. It is only when one has opportunity to compare the shell with a print of 1803 from *The Theatric Tourist*[1] that the truth begins to dawn. The original portico, together with the whole of the nearer part of the building, has been taken away, leaving only the auditorium walls which once included the stage. There are cottages flanking the green on which the theatre looks. The old print shows these as directly adjoining the corners of the theatre. Today these same cottages still exist, but are seen to be some feet away from the theatre, and connected with it by a later brick wall. On the intervening ground the front-of-house offices once stood as seen in the print. It is the lack of these that gives so different an outward appearance to the playhouse. But the square chimneys in the print above the light-coloured façade have left marks on the present end wall, and, though other windows have now been broken out, the body of the building remains.

[1] See Plates 43 and 44.

Inside are few features of interest left. The complete theatre furniture has vanished, but there remains—rather surprisingly—a ceiling that in its way is unique. The plaster is almost ready to fall away from the laths, but it has been shored up with battens and wire net and still, with its faded browns and creams, offers a misty last word to our chapter, for though Richmond retains the furniture of the Georgian playhouse, Newbury alone can render something of the glory of the painted interior. Richmond has been covered with frequent later coats of paint—and in some parts, wall-paper—while Newbury has never been 'done up'. Here is offered, then, our final impression to complete this study of the eighteenth-century playhouse.

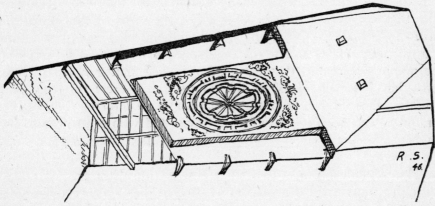

Fig. 19A: Sketch of the painted ceiling at Newbury [*Richard Southern Collection*

Chapter Four

GEORGIAN THEATRES OF THE NINETEENTH CENTURY

Ipswich, 1803—Plymouth, 1811—Newcastle-upon-Tyne, 1837—
Chatsworth—Hereford

THERE REMAINS NOW a postscript to the story. The Georgian era merged into the Regency and a new phase followed again with the Victorians. One theatre especially bore signs of this transition from Georgian to Victorian, and though nothing but part of the outer wall remains today, the one-time playhouse had its story recorded in a unique way by the hand of its last manager, H. R. Eyre, who left a scrapbook of its life for us to see the struggling of a building born at the end of the Georgian phase and true to Georgian tradition, but born too late for its times, and whose life was an unending, and finally unsuccessful, attempt to alter internally and come up to date.

This playhouse was at Ipswich, and was built in 1803 on the site of an older theatre. Of its plan in 1810 Eyre has preserved for us a copy[1]. It was built with the typical Georgian surround of boxes, the typical doors, and the typical three storeys of auditorium. A couple of years after its opening there was built in London a playhouse called the Sans Pareil which, as a print of 1816 shows, had certain new features; of these the most striking was the abolition of the Georgian tier of boxes flanking the pit, and the extension of that pit outwards under what now becomes a raised first circle of the form that we

[1] See Fig. 20.

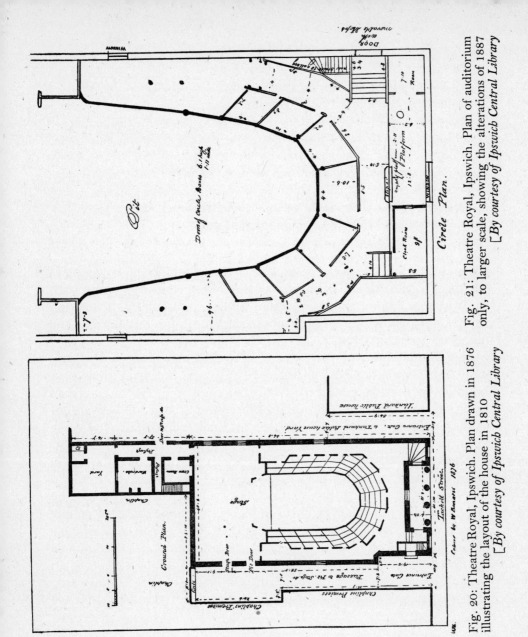

Circle Plan.

Fig. 21: Theatre Royal, Ipswich. Plan of auditorium only, to larger scale, showing the alterations of 1887
[By courtesy of Ipswich Central Library

Fig. 20: Theatre Royal, Ipswich. Plan drawn in 1876 illustrating the layout of the house in 1810
[By courtesy of Ipswich Central Library

see in our older theatres today. This fashion spread to later theatres and created a new era of auditorium design.

Ipswich, however, could not follow this innovation fully since it was limited by its now old-fashioned Georgian skeleton, and a curious hybrid shape was arrived at[1] by which only the 'front boxes' were retained, and the side boxes were stripped of their subdivisions and, in some cases, even of their fronts, and became as it were 'wings' to the pit. This took place in 1887, but the race was unequal. No mere alteration could bring a Georgian playhouse easily to the new fashion of the rising times. In 1890 the die was cast and the erection of a new theatre altogether put an end to the struggles of the old.

The eighty years of its story form a most interesting example of the character of the Georgian playhouse, how individual it was and how considerably it differed from the Victorian. Furthermore, we are in the unusually lucky position of being able very clearly to visualize how the different auditoriums looked at Ipswich, for we possess not only a water-colour of the last state of the Georgian interior in 1885, but—an item of exceptional interest—an actual photograph from the year 1889 of the auditorium as it appeared after the alteration to the boxes, a picture which may claim to be the earliest actual photograph yet known to us of an English theatre interior—certainly the earliest to portray an auditorium still possessing fundamentally Georgian lines[2].

Among the last of the well-recorded late-Regency theatres, place must be kept for Foulston's large conception at Plymouth begun in 1811, which, apart from its general interest to a student of auditorium development, has two other notable features: it presents us with a very fine forerunner of the now-popular conception of a Civic Centre —one nearly a century and a half before its time—and it offers in its plans the fullest details yet discovered of the working of the groove-system of scene-shifting mentioned earlier in this book and vaguely foreshadowed by the curious wooden object found at Bristol[3].

[1] Seen in Fig. 21.   [2] See Plates 45 and 46.   [3] See Plate 1 and p. 21.

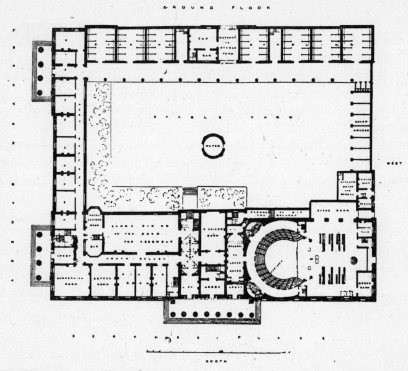

Fig. 22: Theatre Royal, Plymouth. Foulston's plan of 1811 for the complete hotel
square   [*From Foulston's 'Buildings in the West of England'*, 1838

The façade of Foulston's Theatre Royal was still standing in the
first quarter of the present century and it formed part of a grand
scheme including club, dining rooms, assembly room, coffee room,
and a vast hotel with extensive stables, the whole occupying an
island site of some 250 feet by 300 feet. Now all but the columns of
the adjoining Athenaeum has disappeared. The theatre occupied the
north-west corner of the plan, the corner next to the distant
Athenaeum[1].

[1] See Fig. 22 and Plates 47 and 48.

LONGITUDINAL SECTION

ELEVATION OF PRINCIPAL FRONT

Fig. 23: Theatre Royal, Plymouth. Longitudinal section and elevation

[From Foulston

The original auditorium contained tiers of Georgian-style boxes and the traditional proscenium doors. The plans initiate us far more closely than is usual into the secrets of the stage machinery. We see[1] several details of what are known as the 'fly-floors', those working galleries above either side of the stage. Furthermore, above the railing of this gallery we see two of the horizontal shafts on which the lines suspending the borders were wound and, below, a winch controlling the ascent or descent of the traditional cloud-

[1] See Figs. 23, 24 and 25.

machine like those used in the earliest days of the Restoration. At the back of the stage was the painting room, with a counterweighted frame hung so as to be lowered through the floor to enable the scene painter to reach all the parts of the cloth or flats fixed to it.

The fly-rail which guarded this gallery ran right round the stage and thus contained a portion crossing the back of the stage from side to side. On the drawing showing this back-portion is illustrated a front view of the same cloud-machine, but most interesting of all is the apparatus attached under the side floors and projecting horizontally out over the stage. Upon the spectator's right-hand side this apparatus, in the form of a narrow strip, is seen to be hinged in the centre and its projecting end is shown partly pulled up, like a drawbridge.

It was for this purpose that the two strap hinges projecting beyond the end of the Bristol groove were intended. Originally the piece was suspended, grooved surface down, under the fly-floor, and had an extension to the longer part which could be raised out of the way when not required. In the shorter grooves to the right of the piece the heads of scenery-wings used to slide, and in the longer grooves and their extension, now missing, the heads of the 'flats' (as the two halves of the back scene were called) similarly slid, one pair giving place to another as the play proceeded.

The disposition of the various groups of these grooves (of which there would be some four or more pairs to a medium sized stage) is seen in the plan, where the short grooves and long grooves of each group are clearly distinguished.

The theatre at Newcastle-upon-Tyne, designed by John and B. Green, is dated 1837. The façade, with some quality of impressiveness, still remains, but the interior was gutted by fire in 1899. A recent discovery, however, has brought to light a complete set of the original plans, and we may now compare the façade with the

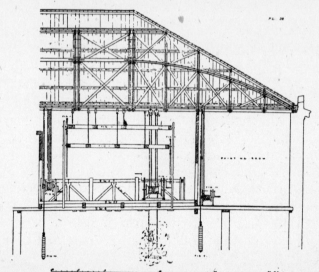

Fig. 24: Theatre Royal, Plymouth. Detail of the fly-floor seen also in Fig. 23
[From Foulston

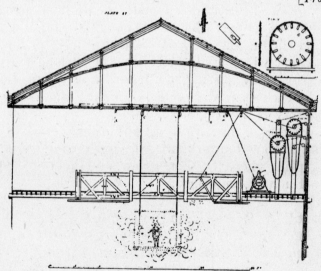

Fig. 25: Theatre Royal, Plymouth. Detail of back section of fly-floor looked at from the proscenium
[From Foulston

architect's design[1] in which a lady in contemporary costume stands with exploratory foot upon the steps between the great columns, and see the disposition and decoration of this early example of the theatres of the early-Victorian period. It still had something of the compact unity of the Georgian houses but its whole conception was more pretentious. It retained a dying manifestation of the Georgian boxes but had a proscenium not only of a new design but of a new intention, for now no proscenium door is seen. The contemporary drama had slid deeper on the stage, and now introduced its characters in the naturalistic manner through the scenery, and no longer in the more conventional earlier way, through the proscenium and on to the fore-stage.

Space has allowed us little comment hitherto on the manners of the Georgian audience, save for a brief note of the smell and the splashes of candle-wax at Bath on page 32; no mention has been made of the brawling in the pit, and only oblique reference to the behaviour in the boxes. The picture, however, gains one touch of horrific relief when we learn that even at Victorian Newcastle in 1837 it was ruled 'that the floor between the front seats and the front of the gallery be covered with lead to prevent nuisances'.

Three pictures now conclude our short review. The first comes near to being too late to include in any survey of the Georgian theatre that should claim to be closely bound by time-limits, for it cannot be earlier than 1823, but to the glimpse of the painted ceiling at Newbury it would be a pity not to add a reproduction of some of the finest old theatrical painting left in England, that on the proscenium of the Duke of Devonshire's private theatre at Chatsworth[2]. Here was an accomplishment of scene-painter's craft that probably informed more of the Georgian playhouse than the ephemeral nature of the materials will allow us easily to realize today. All the elaborate

[1] See Plates 50 and 51, also Plates 52, 53 and 54.   [2] See Plate 49.

architectural embellishment of this stage-front is painted upon the flat with a skill and a sense of amusement in the task that must have graced much of the scene painting of the previous century. Some echo of the achievements may come to us yet from old play-bills, but here is an example of the quality of the thing itself that is too rarely come by, at any rate in England, to miss.

The final two pictures carry a sharp hortation to all would-be investigators. They show a theatre that, it seems, can never now be studied. It was pulled down in Hereford in 1937. The photographs remain[1], but we are ten years too late now to examine the building. Little has yet been found of its history. The theatre was called the Alhambra and it is said to have been built in the reign of William IV.

In the eighties it was used as a concert- and music-hall and it once formed part of the Royal Oak Inn. The photograph of the stage seems doubtfully to present the remains of proscenium doorways, but no suggestion whatever is to be found of boxes or sunk pit. Had the theatre been surveyed in its time we might possess further evidence on the late-Regency auditorium to round off our story, but we are too late. As it is we must leave our survey in this atmosphere of decay and demolition but with the encouraging note that the interest of this unique branch of theatrical development, the Playhouse of Georgian Britain, is at length beginning to receive the study it deserves as a particular manifestation of the national genius and that, though this comes too late to save Plymouth or to study Hereford, yet it arrives in time to take informed and sympathetic interest in such records as remain and, we may hope, to add to them very soon with discoveries of others up till now hidden.

To that end may this preliminary study contribute its share.

[1] See Plates 55 and 56.

THE PLATES

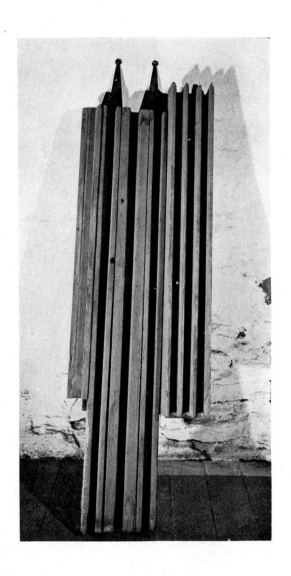

PLATE 1: The English Theatrical Groove

PLATE 2: Wren's Sectional Drawing, presumed for Drury Lane, 1674

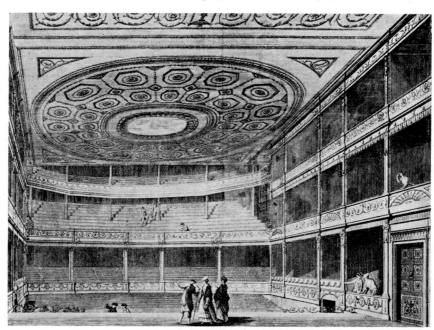

PLATE 3: The Adams' Redecoration of Drury Lane, 1775

PLATE 4: Drury Lane in 1792

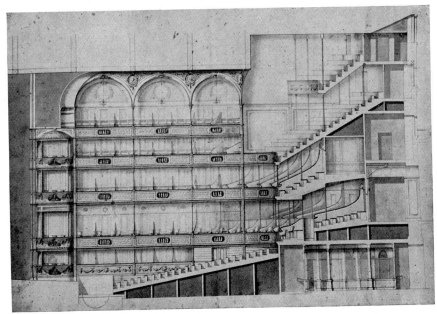

PLATE 5: Holland's Drury Lane, 1794

PLATE 6: The Royalty Theatre, Wellclose Square, 1787

PLATE 7: Auditorium of the Royalty Theatre in 1794

PLATE 8: The Royalty Theatre as redecorated in 1815

PLATE 9: Auditorium of the Royalty Theatre in 1815

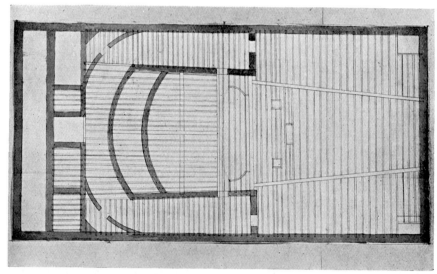

PLATE 10: Basement plan attributed to Royalty Theatre

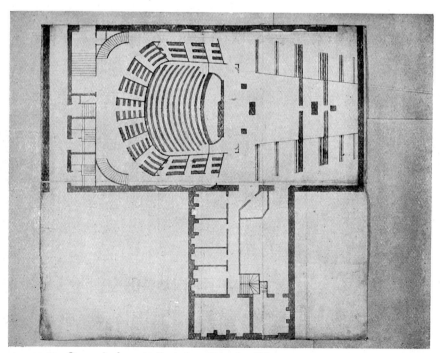

PLATE 11: Ground plan attributed to Royalty Theatre

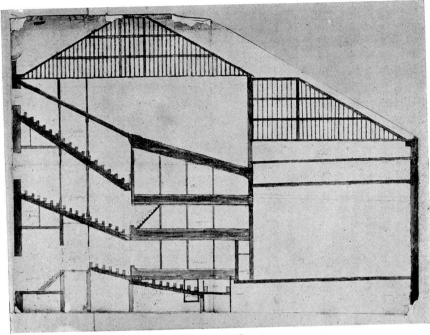

PLATE 12: Section attributed to Royalty Theatre

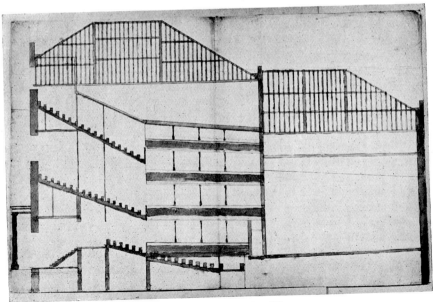

PLATE 13: Second section attributed to Royalty Theatre

PLATE 14: The Theatre Royal, Orchard Street, Bath, 1750

PLATE 15: Interior of Theatre Royal, Orchard Street, Bath

PLATE 16: The Theatre Royal, Beauford Square, Bath, 1805

PLATE 17: Geo. Dance's sketch for the Beauford Square façade

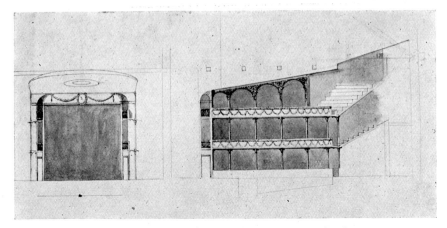

PLATE 18: Dance's drawings for the Beauford Square auditorium

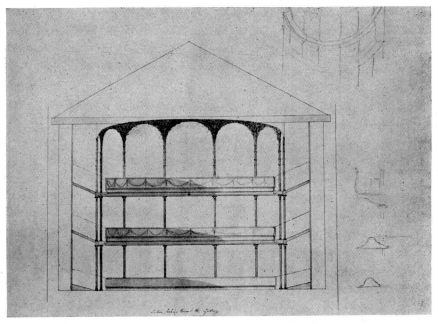

PLATE 19: Cross-section of Beauford Square auditorium

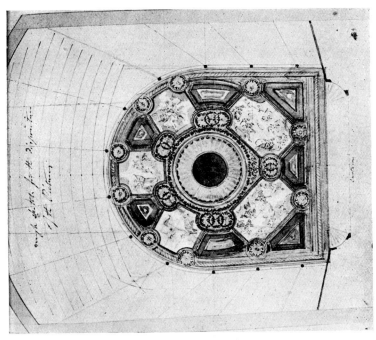

PLATE 21: Sketch plan of Beauford Square ceiling

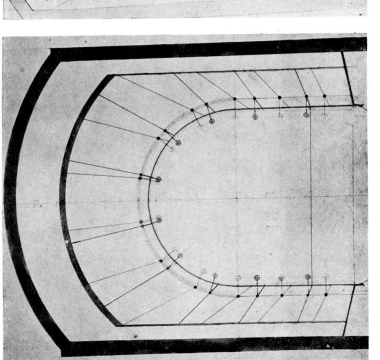

PLATE 20: Plan of Beauford Square pit and boxes

PLATE 22: The Theatre Royal, Bristol, 1766. The auditorium

PLATE 23: The Theatre Royal, Bristol. The side boxes

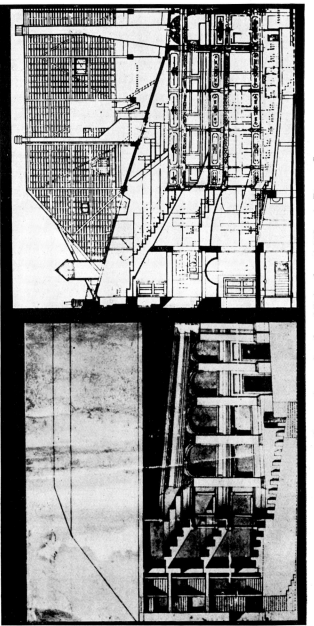

PLATE 24: Comparison of scale of Bristol and Wren's Drury Lane

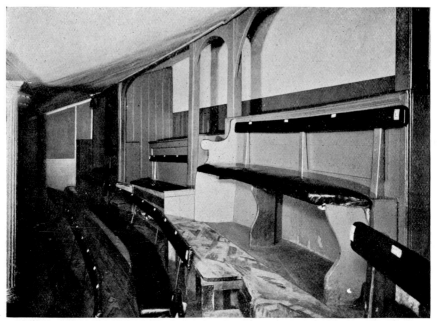

PLATE 25: The Theatre Royal, Bristol. In the old upper side boxes

PLATE 26: Georgian decoration revealed under Victorian ornament, Bristol

PLATE 28: The Pit Passage, Bristol

PLATE 27: The auditorium ceiling, Bristol

PLATE 29: The Backstage Recess, Bristol

PLATE 30: Machinery under the stage, Bristol

PLATE 31: The Thunder-run in the loft, Bristol

PLATE 32: The Theatre at Stamford, Lincs, 1768

PLATE 33: Door discovered in cellar of Stamford Theatre

PLATE 34: The Theatre at Richmond, Yorkshire, 1788

PLATE 36: Paybox at Richmond, Yorkshire

PLATE 35: Entrance Door at Richmond, Yorkshire

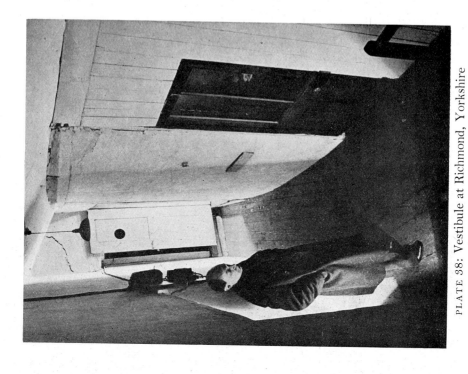

PLATE 38: Vestibule at Richmond, Yorkshire

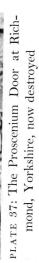

PLATE 37: The Proscenium Door at Richmond, Yorkshire, now destroyed

PLATE 39: The Theatre at Richmond, Yorkshire, before reclamation

PLATE 40: Model Reconstruction of Richmond Theatre, Yorkshire

PLATE 41: Stage at Richmond, Yorkshire, from gallery

PLATE 42: Stage at Richmond, Yorkshire, from side boxes

PLATE 43: The Theatre at Newbury, Berks, opened 1802

PLATE 44: Newbury Theatre from a print of 1803

PLATE 45: Watercolour of Ipswich Theatre painted in 1885

PLATE 46: Ipswich Theatre from a photograph of 1889

PLATE 47: The Theatre Royal, Plymouth, opened 1813

PLATE 48: Print of Theatre Royal, Plymouth

PLATE 49: The Duke of Devonshire's Private Theatre at Chatsworth

PLATE 50: The Theatre Royal, Newcastle-upon-Tyne, opened 1837

PLATE 51: Green's design for Newcastle façade

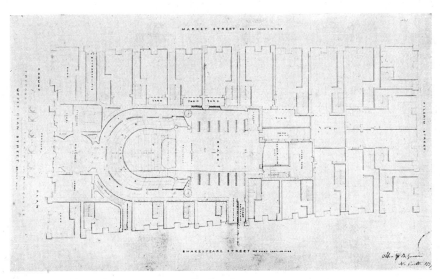

PLATE 52: Green's plan for Newcastle Theatre

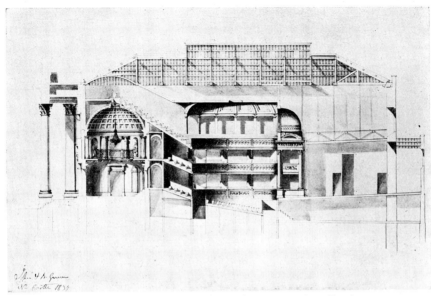

PLATE 53: Longitudinal section of Newcastle stage and auditorium

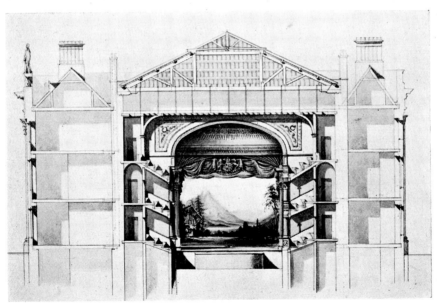

PLATE 54: Cross-section of Newcastle auditorium showing proscenium

PLATE 55: Auditorium of the Alhambra, Hereford, now destroyed   [*Wyeval*

PLATE 56: Stage of the Alhambra, Hereford   [*Wyeval*

NOTES ON THE PLATES

Plate 1: THE ENGLISH THEATRICAL GROOVE
At the Theatre Royal, Bristol, there was found a few years ago the earliest known surviving remnant of the unique English groove system of scene changing. This system obtained from the time of Inigo Jones to that of Irving. It was never widely used outside England, but closely suited the English type of play in many short, quick-changing scenes. No understanding of the form of the British drama is possible without some acquaintance with the working of this machine, for which see pp. 21 and 59.

Plate 2: WREN'S SECTIONAL DRAWING (PRESUMED) FOR DRURY LANE, 1674
The earliest known architectural drawing of the interior of an English playhouse. This building was frequently altered and was finally demolished as outmoded in 1792.   *[All Souls' College, Oxford*

Plate 3: THE ADAMS' REDECORATION OF DRURY LANE IN 1775
The same house as Pl. 2, but showing the Adam Brothers' new design for the auditorium. All the decoration shown here is painted on the flat.
[Richard Southern Collection

Plate 4: DRURY LANE IN 1792
The same house again as Pl. 2. Greenwood and Capon redecorated the Adams' interior of Wren's Drury Lane in 1783, and this house was finally demolished to make room for a bigger theatre in 1792.
[Print from a drawing by William Capon. Richard Southern Collection

Plate 5: HOLLAND'S DRURY LANE, 1794
An architectural section for the building which replaced Wren's Drury Lane, and was one of the largest theatres in British history.
[Courtesy of the Trustees of Sir John Soane's Museum

Plate 6: THE ROYALTY THEATRE, WELLCLOSE SQUARE. THE STAGE 1787
[Common Ground Collection

[65]   H

Plate 7: THE ROYALTY THEATRE, WELLCLOSE SQUARE. THE AUDITORIUM, 1794
[*Richard Southern Collection*

Plate 8: THE ROYALTY THEATRE, WELLCLOSE SQUARE. THE STAGE IN 1815
[*Common Ground Collection*

Plate 9: THE ROYALTY THEATRE, WELLCLOSE SQUARE. THE AUDITORIUM IN 1815
Comparison of Pls. 8 and 9 with Pls. 6 and 7 opposite gives a good idea of the
trend of taste in decoration which marked the development of a typical, simple
Georgian auditorium to one in the more ornate Regency style—itself a forecast of
the Early Victorian profusion.   [*Common Ground Collection*

Plate 10: DRAWING ASCRIBED TO THE ROYALTY THEATRE
A plan of the basement walls of the stage, auditorium and lobbies showing the
position of the floor joists. The plan of the pit passage is well shown either side,
with the entrance to the pit opening from the side, and the door to the understage
machine room at the end.   [*Enthoven Collection*

Plate 11: DRAWING INSCRIBED 'THE GROUND PLAN OF THE ROYALTY THEATRE, 1786'
Though the date agrees with that of the Royalty Theatre, Wellclose Square, these
four plans bear no relation to the appearance of the house as shown in Pls. 6 to 9,
and their connection with that building needs verifying. This plate shows a ground
plan of the whole building.   [*Enthoven Collection*

Plate 12: SECTION ASCRIBED TO THE ROYALTY THEATRE
This drawing shows an arrangement of three tiers. The upper gallery is inscribed
'1st Gallery', and the lower '2nd Gallery', which is unusual.
[*Enthoven Collection*

Plate 13: SECOND SECTION ASCRIBED TO THE ROYALTY THEATRE
Showing an auditorium in four tiers, but with a flatter ceiling. These drawings
bear, inscribed on the back, the names of Cornelius Dixon and William Capon.
They are crudely executed in brown and yellow.
[*Enthoven Collection*

[66]

Plate 14: THE THEATRE ROYAL, ORCHARD STREET, BATH, 1750
The existing shell of the old theatre. Interior now altered for a Freemasons' hall.
[*National Buildings Record*

Plate 15: INTERIOR OF THE ORCHARD STREET THEATRE, BATH
From a watercolour by Nixon, now inaccessible but reproduced in Mowbray
Green's *The Eighteenth Century Architecture of Bath.*

Plate 16: THE THEATRE ROYAL, BEAUFORD SQUARE, BATH, 1805
[*National Buildings Record*

Plate 17: DANCE'S SKETCH FOR BEAUFORD SQUARE FAÇADE
One of two rough projects by Geo. Dance for this building. Compare with Pl. 16.
[*Courtesy of the Trustees of Sir John Soane's Museum*

Plates 18–21: AUDITORIUM DESIGNS FOR BEAUFORD SQUARE, BATH
The building was put up by Palmer, interior and façade by Geo. Dance. Pl. 18, an
elevation of the proscenium and a longitudinal section through the auditorium.
Pl. 19, elevation of end of auditorium, with slight sketch showing ceiling (compare
Pls. 20 and 21 and Fig. 3). Pl. 20, plan of the lower boxes showing experiments
in arranging the partitions, columns and the lights hanging therefrom. Pl. 21,
rough sketch for the disposition of the Cassali pictures in the general ceiling
design.
[*Courtesy of the Trustees of Sir John Soane's Museum*

Plate 22: THE THEATRE ROYAL, BRISTOL, 1766
The oldest surviving playhouse in Britain retaining features of the original form.
The interior has been frequently redecorated. For plan and section see Figs. 14
and 15. [*Arts Council*

Plate 23: THE THEATRE ROYAL, BRISTOL
View of the proscenium side and boxes specially taken for comparison with the
theatre in Pl. 2, upon which it was closely modelled.
[*National Buildings Record*

Plate 24: THE THEATRE ROYAL, BRISTOL

A comparison between the auditorium of Wren's Drury Lane and that at Bristol, reproduced to the same scale. [*Richard Southern Collection*

Plate 25: THE THEATRE ROYAL, BRISTOL

A view inside the one-time boxes of the middle tier. Traces of the old partitions still remain.

Plate 26: THE THEATRE ROYAL, BRISTOL

A detail of the auditorium showing where the Victorian decoration over the columns has been taken away, revealing the Georgian classic architectural motifs underneath. The whole auditorium probably possesses a complete scheme of Georgian panelling, etc., under the later canvas and plaster ornaments.

Plate 27: THE THEATRE ROYAL, BRISTOL

Looking up at the auditorium ceiling. The gallery front at the back of the theatre is just seen in the bottom of the picture. The section at the top is directly over the forestage.

Plate 28: THE THEATRE ROYAL, BRISTOL

View of the Pit Passage, leading from the front of the house under the side boxes. Looking towards the door to the under-stage machine room.

Plate 29: THE THEATRE ROYAL, BRISTOL

The recess at the back of the stage.

Plate 30: THE THEATRE ROYAL, BRISTOL

A view of the under-stage machinery taken from just within the door shown in Pl. 28.

Plate 31: THE THEATRE ROYAL, BRISTOL

The loft above the auditorium. The wooden case to the lower left is over the central grille of the ceiling in Pl. 27. To the extreme right is the wall separating auditorium from stage. The two diagonal timbers spanning the space from top-right to left-of-centre, and thence to centre-bottom are the hollow troughs of the thunder-run.

Plate 32: THE THEATRE AT STAMFORD, LINCOLNSHIRE, 1768

The façade of a building whose interior is now entirely transformed to a modern clubroom. *[Courtesy of the Marquess of Exeter*

Plate 33: DOOR FROM STAMFORD THEATRE

This door was found by the author in the cellar and is most likely one of the old proscenium doors from the stage. If so it is probably the last remaining contemporary example of its kind in Britain. See also Fig. 16.

[Courtesy of the Marquess of Exeter

Plate 34: THE THEATRE AT RICHMOND, YORKSHIRE, 1788

The exterior from the north, showing entrance door at the side.

Plate 35: THE THEATRE AT RICHMOND, YORKS

Detail of entrance showing wall inside at foot of stairs which once contained the entrance to the pit passage.

Plate 36: THE THEATRE AT RICHMOND, YORKS

The paybox.

Plate 37: THE THEATRE AT RICHMOND, YORKS

A photograph taken during the use of the building as a wartime salvage depot, showing the proscenium side and the door in place. The door is now unfortunately destroyed and this photograph is possibly the only one in existence to show a Georgian proscenium door in position. For relation with rest of auditorium compare Pl. 40.

Plate 38: THE THEATRE AT RICHMOND, YORKS
The vestibule or lobby.

Plate 39: THE THEATRE AT RICHMOND, YORKS

An old view taken before its reclamation, after a period of use as a corn-chandler's store.

Plate 40: MODEL RECONSTRUCTION OF THE RICHMOND (YORKS) THEATRE

Model constructed from evidence in the fabric of the building by J. Neville Terry and Richard Southern of the probable original appearance of the interior, with the sloping pit restored.

Plate 41: THE THEATRE AT RICHMOND, YORKS

View of the stage from the gallery taken to show as much of the floor as belonged to the original stage area. Compare with Fig. 9 showing intimacy achieved between actor and audience by this arrangement of deep fore-stage.

Plate 42: THE THEATRE AT RICHMOND, YORKS

View of the stage from the side boxes. That part of the present floor which was originally pit-space is covered with a black cloth. Measured details of this building are to be found in Figs. 17, 18 and 19.

Plate 43: THE THEATRE AT NEWBURY, BERKS, 1802
The exterior in 1946, compare with Pl. 44.

Plate 44: NEWBURY THEATRE IN 1803
Print showing the original façade and portico, now pulled down. The cottages either side still remain. *[Richard Southern Collection*

Plate 45: THEATRE ROYAL, IPSWICH, BUILT 1805

From a watercolour by the resident scene-painter, William Burgess, made in 1885. For plan see Fig. 20.   *[Ipswich Central Library*

Plate 46: THEATRE ROYAL, IPSWICH

Interior from a photograph of 1889—possibly the earliest photograph of an English auditorium at present known. For plan see Fig. 21.

[Ipswich Central Library

Plate 47: THE THEATRE ROYAL, PLYMOUTH, OPENED 1813

From an old photograph about 1890. The building was demolished in the late 1930s, but the columns of the Athenaeum (see at right-hand edge) still remain though badly damaged by air raids.

Plate 48: THE THEATRE ROYAL, PLYMOUTH

A print of Foulston's building housing a sort of Georgian 'civic centre'. The theatre was in the farther section of the building beyond the portico. For plans see Figs. 22 and 23.   *[Richard Southern Collection*

Plate 49: THE PRIVATE THEATRE AT CHATSWORTH

The Duke of Devonshire's Private Theatre offers a fine example of effective scene-painting, the whole proscenium being of flat painted canvas with the relief achieved merely by skilful brushwork.   *[Courtesy of the Duke of Devonshire*

Plate 50: THEATRE ROYAL, NEWCASTLE-UPON-TYNE

This façade still exists from Green's 1837 design which has recently been discovered and may be compared in Pl. 51. The interior of the present building is modern.   *[National Buildings Record*

Plate 51: GREEN'S PLANS FOR NEWCASTLE 1837. ELEVATION
[Metropolitan Museum of Art, New York

Plate 52: GREEN'S GROUND PLAN FOR NEWCASTLE THEATRE ROYAL
[*Metropolitan Museum of Art, New York*

Plate 53: LONGITUDINAL SECTION THROUGH GREEN'S NEWCASTLE AUDITORIUM

This drawing was reproduced with a short account in *Theatre Notebook* No. 2, January–March, 1946. The remaining three are here reproduced for the first time.
[*Metropolitan Museum of Art, New York*

Plate 54: CROSS-SECTION THROUGH GREEN'S NEWCASTLE AUDITORIUM
[*Metropolitan Museum of Art, New York*

Plate 55: THE ALHAMBRA, HEREFORD. AUDITORIUM

Plate 56: THE ALHAMBRA, HEREFORD. STAGE